IRONCLAD LETTERS

FOR GODLY BOYS, YOUNG MEN & MEN DIFFERENCE MAKERS

by Crystal N. White, M.A., LPC

Ironclad Letters for Godly Boys, Young Men and Men

ISBN: 979-8-9947986-2-1

Cover and book designed by Crystal N. White.
Published by Crystal N. White.
Printed in the USA.
First printing edition 2026.
Images used with permission for commercial use.
http://www.psalmlifestyle.com
customersupport@cnw.life

ABOUT THE AUTHOR

Crystal N. White, is an author, Licensed Professional Counselor (LPC) and Life Transformation and Emotional Intelligence Life Coach. She received her Bachelors of Arts in Communication Studies-Interpersonal and Public from the University of Missouri-Kansas City. She went on to receive her Masters of Arts in Counseling from MidAmerica Nazarene University, Olathe, Kansas.

Crystal is the founder, Chair, and President/CEO of Raise and Revive Community Garden, NFP (RRCG) a nonprofit in its early stages of development. RRCG's goal, "To be a charitable organization that promotes holistic health care by connecting underserved communities with community resources, spiritual support and affordable and accessible case management and counseling services."

Her personal mission is to encourage people to live with intention and purpose to meet the needs of their community by using their God-given gifts, talents and uniqueness. Her goal is to use the arts to empower people to seek and know God and the Bible for themselves.

Please be blessed by these other books available on Crystal's website and Amazon: ®
Jewel Letters for Godly Girls, Young Women & Women (2026)
PSALM Strategy Journal for Marriage (2026)
PSALM Strategy Journal for Mental and Emotional Healing (2026)
Lacking Nothing Psalm 23: The Lord is My Shepherd, I Lack Nothing, Vol. 1 (2018)
Yours, Truly: A Novel (2013)

www.psalmlifestyle.com

THANK YOU

Follow Crystal On Social Media

@crystalforwholeness

@Crystal4whlness

@crystalforwholeness3996

CONTENTS

Letter One: Methuselah
A Legacy Carrier p. 6

Letter Two: Adam
The First Man to be Fruitful and Multiply p. 17

Letter Three: Joseph
An Example of Overcoming Temptation p. 26

Letter Four: Zacchaeus
An Example of Repentance p. 35

Letter Five: John the Baptist
Prophet and Priest p. 44

Letter Six: King David
A Good Friend p. 52

Letter Seven: Boaz
A Kinsman-Redemer p. 61

Letter Eight: Aquila
A Husband in Ministry with His Wife p. 68

Letter Nine: Moses
Prophet, Lawgiver, Mediator p. 75

Letter Ten: Elijah
A Witness that God is Our Source p. 83

Difference Maker Mindset
Think. Be. Connect. Do. p. 93

Letter Eleven: Your Letter
You are a Difference Maker, too! p. 109

IRONCLAD LETTERS

FOR GODLY BOYS, YOUNG MEN & MEN
DIFFERENCE MAKERS

THE ARMOR OF GOD MAKES A MAN VICTORIOUS.

IN CHRIST, YOU ARE AN IRONCLAD MAN.

Strength is the trait people want to possess because strength gets them through the tough times. Strength is needed to start a task and see it to the end. There are two kinds of strength a man can possess: One, strength in himself and his own abilities but this strength will grow weary and sometimes lead to abandoning the assignment. Two, the strength of God empowers a man to be strong even when he grows weary, to have hope when things get heavy or when there's no end in sight to the suffering, he remains steadfast. The strength of God keeps carrying that man through every season, test and trial. The latter of the two entails a spiritual armor, the armor of God that makes a righteous man an "ironclad man."

Ephesians 6:6-12

"Finally, be strong in the LORD and in His mighty power. Put on the full armor of God, so that you can take your stand against the devil's schemes. For our struggle is not against flesh and blood, but against the rulers, against the authorities, against the powers of this dark world and against the spiritual forces of evil in the heavenly realms. Therefore, put on the full armor of God, so that when the day of evil comes, you may be able to stand your ground, and after you have done everything, to stand. Stand firm then, with the belt of truth buckled around your waist, with the breastplate of righteousness in place, and with your feet fitted with the readiness that comes from the gospel of peace. In addition to all this, take up the shield of faith, with which you can extinguish all the flaming arrows of the evil one. Take the helmet of salvation and the sword of the Spirit, which is the word of God."

Ironclad means, "sheathed (an object fitted with something to preserve it) in armor"; "so firm or secure as to be unbreakable" and "having no obvious weakness" (Merriam-Webster, n.d). The armor of God shields and protects a righteous man in every battle, making him more than a conqueror and an overcomer. The armor in Ephesians 6 makes the ironclad man stand firm, secure and unbreakable in Christ Jesus. There's no weakness in the armor of God because it's the mighty power of God strengthening a man to stand against the schemes of the devil and pull-down strongholds. This workbook was created to remind you in Christ you'll win every battle if you're wearing the armor of God. In Christ, you are an ironclad man covered in the armor of God.

My brother, I want you to know that the "weapons of our warfare are not carnal, but they are mighty in God in pulling down strongholds" (2 Corinthians 10:4). God is calling ironclad men like yourself to rise up, use the armor of God to be the salt in the earth, proclaiming the good news. I want you to know you're a Difference Maker even if you don't believe it. Since Christ is in you, you're a Difference Maker even if you don't feel like one. The light of Christ shines so brightly in you, you can do impossible things through God if you just believe. If you happen to be unsure of the impact your life can have, I'm hoping when you complete this workbook you believe and start to live like: A DIFFERENCE MAKER READY TO SHINE!

YOU AND YOUR GIFTS ARE NEEDED IN YOUR COMMUNITY AND IN THE WORLD.

I hope to motivate and empower you to embrace the "Difference Maker Mindset" as you work with your hands. In the Bible Paul says living such a life wins the respect of outsiders, people who don't believe in Christ. Living your life with the Difference Maker Mindset will show people around you that the LORD God Almighty who lives in you, is God.

The goal of this workbook is to give you information so you can know what the Bible says about you, the call to tell others about Christ, and to believe and live boldly as the Difference Maker you are in Christ Jesus.

This workbook has ten sections called "letters" that'll lead you into a study of ten men in the Bible. Their stories will showcase their impactful lives. You'll read of men like King David who displayed the fruits of the Spirit, loved his enemies and was loyal to a friend, sharing his possessions with the weak. And Methusaleh who led a righteous life before God. These men impacted their community in major ways. These men are our role models who show us how to use our faith, gifts, talents and energy to serve God and our community in our daily lives. Their lives express the strength of God and selfless action that made their community successful.

In this workbook you and the Biblical men are called "Ironclad Men." At the end of each section, you'll write a personal letter to each ironclad man. In this letter you'll talk about how he inspired you to be a Difference Maker in your community, home, school and work. I hope through these letters you'll discover or re-discover the valuable and wonderful talents, gifts and energy God has blessed you with so you can share it with others.

God creates everything for a purpose including you. If you happen to be dealing with insecurity or low self-esteem, by the end of this study I'm hoping you go from thinking "I can't do it" to "I can do it" then to "I'm doing it."

And whatever your "it" is you know it's significance. The world needs your light.

GOAL FOR THIS WORKBOOK:

To inspire you to use your gifts and talents to be a Difference Maker in your community.

3 OBJECTIVES TO REACH THIS GOAL:

Learn the traits of men who lived ironclad lives as the light of Christ shone through them.

Learn what the Bible says about living like Christ and how to practice Christ's ways in your daily interactions with others.

Learn and use the Difference Maker Mindset to put your faith into action, working with your hands to impact your community for Christ.

LET'S GET TO WORK DIFFERENCE MAKER!

The men in this workbook are the stories of Biblical men whose stories are just like ours-stories of pain, purpose, joy, sadness, sin, fear, boldness, faith, trust, uncertainty, loss, love and victory. God walked with them, showing Himself strong on their behalf. His protection, love and principles guided them. Each Biblical man was a Difference Maker in the time he was graced to be on the earth. His life has a lesson locked in it that we're going to study and learn from.

These men were Difference Makers who are forerunners chosen by God to glorify Him in the earth. As these men were called during their time, this is your time. You're now being called by God to rise up, to be a Difference Maker, serving your community and bringing the kingdom of God to unbelievers.

As previously stated, this workbook is broken into sections called, "letters." The letters will have the following:

- The Ironclad Man's Trait page (male figure being studied) to learn about his story and how he responded to the situation presented to him.
- An Ironclad Man Is... guides you into aligning the identified traits of the ironclad man with scripture for your understanding of the traits of a godly man according to the Bible.
- Discussion Questions designed for deeper study of godly traits to know God more. This will help you identify how God shows up in every situation pertaining to a godly man and boy, glorifying Himself in his life.
- Living like Christ page encourages you to learn scriptures and practice the behavior of Christ in your daily life.
- The Difference Maker Mindset section is for you to begin to plan how you're going to put your faith into action by serving your community with your gifts and talents. You'll examine your natural and spiritual gifts, consider your talents, interests, hobbies and passions to jumpstart your involvement in community service to make a difference in your community.
- Letter Eleven, the final letter is your letter. This is for mapping your traits to align them with Christ's image. Celebrate yourself and your uniqueness as God's son, His masterpiece.

The New International Version (NIV) of the Bible was used to create this study. It is recommended you use the NIV to complete your workbook as the questions line up with this version of the Bible. Parts of the workbook will be modified for boys ages 11-13. The modification will be designated with ● .

This is an in-depth study of the Bible so please plan to take your time, giving yourself 4-8 weeks to work through the workbook.

LETTER ONE

METHUSELAH

METHUSELAH

SERVED THE COMMUNITY AS:

A LEGACY CARRIER

Strong Traits: Righteous, Worshipper, Legacy

Methuselah's name meaning in Hebrew:
"Man of the dart" or "Man of the weapon"

Lesson: A righteous man builds an altar and worships the LORD God Almighty only. He teaches his sons and daughters to do the same, leaving a legacy of Christ-followers who shine the light of Christ wherever they go.

Write the definition of each word.

RIGHTEOUS	WORSHIPPER	LEGACY

Read Genesis 4:25-26 and Genesis 5:1-2. Seth was the son God gave Adam and Eve after Abel died. Then Seth had a son named "Enosh." What does Genesis 4:26 say people began to do?

Read Genesis 5:3-32, the bloodline of Adam to Noah then to Abram. Complete the family tree to see the legacy Methuselah carried.

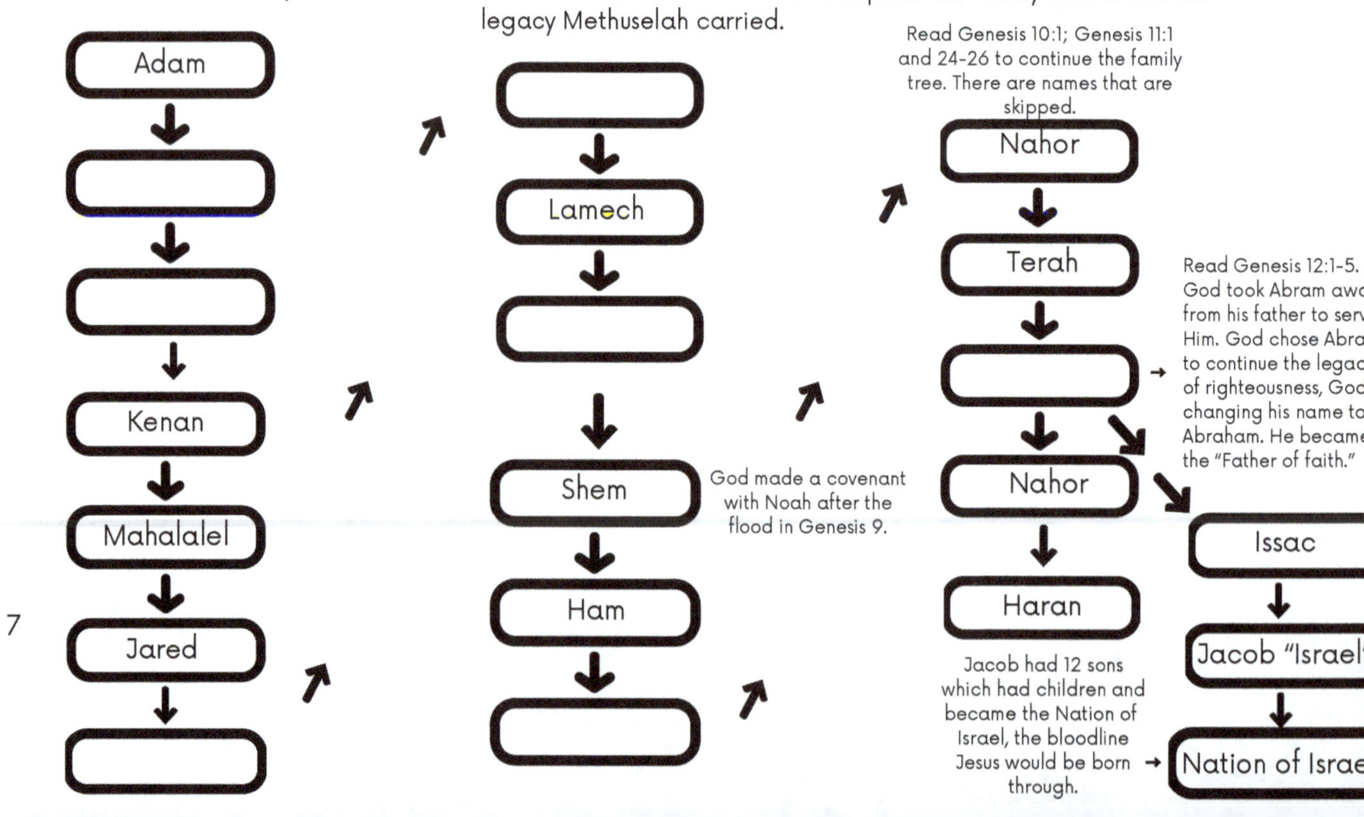

AN IRONCLAD MAN IS...

RIGHTEOUS. A WORSHIPPER. A LEGACY CARRIER.

A righteous man knows in his mind and lives with this in his heart: God is the One True God and beside Him there is no other. An ironclad man is aware of the territory assigned to him. Called and chosen, he governs that territory, never losing sight that Jesus is the First and Last; God is Elohim, the Supreme One. Jesus comes first in a righteous man's heart. He lays his ego down daily on the altar of the Alpha and the Omega. Therefore, he worships King Jesus first and avoids idolatry. He teaches his family and community to do the same, positioning himself for God to establish the legacy He pre-destined him to carry in the earth.

READ EACH VERSE. **WRITE THE SCRIPTURES IN THE BLANK SPACE.**

Righteous

Isaiah 33:15-17

Worshipper

Psalm 95:6

Legacy

Proverbs 20:7

Proverbs 13:22

Building an altar for the LORD: Living a life of worshipping God

Read John 4:24

In your study you see the successful men were the men who were in covenant with God. The response of the men being in covenant with God was to build an altar to God, dedicating his life to worshipping God. Building an altar today symbolizes a place of worship, sacrifice and remembering His goodness. Today the LORD tells us to "worship Him in Spirit and in truth (John 4:24).

As a man, the covenant God enters with you not only determines your success in life and your inheritance of eternal life through Jesus Christ, but your sons and daughters depend on you to be a father, who walks faithfully with the LORD for their own success and salvation. Your sons and daughters depend on a father who'll model walking faithfully with God and teaching them to do so as well. Enoch was Methuselah's father. He walked so faithfully with God he didn't experience death. God took him away (Genesis 5:24). Imagine being Methuselah and seeing your father live a life that was so pleasing to God that He took him away! Methuselah continued to carry his father's legacy, serving the LORD. Methuselah is the longest person to live in the Bible, 969 years! Methuselah raised his son Lamech and became the grandfather of Noah; the man God chose to build an ark and start a whole new world under a new covenant with. Methuselah is an ancestor to Abraham. What a legacy!

DISCUSSION QUESTIONS

 These questions are designed for a deeper personal study or group discussion for ages 11 years old and up.

Use your Notes page for extra writing space.
If you do this with a group discuss your answers.

Although we live in this natural world our spiritual Father reigns on the throne, Creator of heaven and earth. He is the God who created you in His image. This study will teach you or be a review of God's names in Hebrew. A name for a man is his legacy. When someone hears your name, they attach your contribution and your family's contribution to your community and/or the world. As you're building your name, your legacy, remember there is no name above the name of Jesus and, "...that at the name of Jesus every knee should bow, of those in heaven, and of those on earth, and of those under the earth, and that every tongue should confess that Jesus Christ is LORD, to the glory of God the Father" (Philippians 2:10-11). As a man who lives righteously and walks faithfully with your God, call upon God's name in worship, giving honor and respect for Him. Teach your sons and daughters to worship so your family name is known for exalting the name of Jesus to the glory of the Father.

Elohim "Supreme, Mighty One." Genesis 1:1; 1:26-27. What does this teach you about God? Write 1-2 sentences worshipping God as Elohim based on the scriptures you read.

El Shaddai "God Almighty." Genesis 35:1-14. What does this teach you about God? Write 1-2 sentences worshipping God as El Shaddai based on the scriptures you read.

Jehovah Hoseenu "The LORD our Maker." Genesis 1:26-28 and Psalm 95:1-7. What does this teach you about God? Write 1-2 sentences worshipping God as Jehovah Hoseenu based on the scriptures you read.

Adonai "LORD or Master." Exodus 3:14-15, Exodus 6:2-7 Revelation 1:8, Isaiah 45:22 and Psalm 90:2. What does this teach you about God? How do these scriptures teach us to respect God?

DISCUSSION QUESTIONS

These questions are designed for a deeper personal study or group discussion for ages 11 years old and up. If you're doing this study individually, write your answers.

Use your Notes page for extra writing space.

Jehovah El-Mishpat "The God of Justice." Read Isaiah 30:18 and Psalm 89:14-18. What does this teach you about God? How will He show up for you when you need Him?

Abba "Father." Read Mark 14:36 and Romans 8:14-17. What does this teach you about God? How will He show up for you when you need Him?

Jehovah Jireh "The LORD will Provide." Read Genesis 22:1-19. What does this teach you about God? How will He show up for you when you need Him?

Jehovah Rapha "I am the LORD that Heals." Read Psalm 103:1-5. What does this teach you about God? How will He show up for you when you need Him?

Malki-Tzedek often transliterated as Melchizedek "King of Righteousness." Read Genesis 14:17-20. Notice God gave Abram ability to be victorious over his enemies. What does verse 20 say Abram gave the king of Salem? Read Malachi 3:10, Leviticus 27:30 and Proverbs 3:9-10. Summarize what the LORD says about the tithe.

NOTES

You're a Legacy Carrier

"A good man leaves an inheritance to his children's children, but sinner's wealth is laid up for the righteous." (Proverbs 13:22)

This section is for you to pray about building a legacy for your sons and daughters who glorify the LORD on the earth even after your time is over.
The following scriptures bring guidance to fathers for building legacy in Christ.
These are references for you to write a letter of how you plan to build a legacy for your family.
Pray God will reveal to you (if he hasn't already) His will for you and your family. Use this space and the next page to write a letter to yourself, your commitment to your children (or future children and grandchildren) and grandchildren, laying out the plan to leave a legacy as instructed by scripture. You can also use additional scriptures if you want.

Read: Psalm 103:17, Proverbs 22:6, 3 John 1:4, Proverbs 13:3, Deuteronomy 6:5-7, Psalm 112:1-3, Psalm 145:4, Psalm 78:1-8, Matthew 6:19-21.

For godly boys: Read Proverbs 18:21. This scripture means you have the power to curse or bless someone. How you speak over yourself and others especially your children in the future determines how they will see themselves. Even the name you choose for your child sets a destiny in motion for them. Lamech, Noah's father named him "Noah" saying, "He will comfort us in the labor and painful toil of our hands caused by the ground the LORD has cursed" (Genesis 5:29). Noah's name means in Hebrew "rest" or "comfort." We just learned about Noah's destiny and how God made sure Noah lived up to his name.
Write a list of characteristics you want to model for your future sons and daughters. Think of it like this, "When I have children and they are not with me, I want them to act in this manner and or say these things because they saw me doing them and saying them." Use the Godly Values and Characteristics list on page 14 to help you write the values and characters you already have and the ones you want to have as you grow as a man.

You're a Legacy Carrier Cont'd

"A good man leaves an inheritance to his children's children, but sinner's wealth is laid up for the righteous."
(Proverbs 13:22)

Godly Values and Characteristics of a Righteous Man

This list doesn't include all values and characteristics. You can use them and find your own.

Values are standards you live by that determine how you act. They are beliefs that are important and useful to your success.

Accountability
Equality
Security
Ethics
Justice
Authenticity
Financial
Legacy
Simplicity
Self-discipline
Adaptability
Excellence
Kindness
Self-expression
Adventure
Fairness
Knowledge
Self-respect
Faith
Leadership
Ambition
Family
Learning
Service
Diversity
Integrity
Responsibility
Discernment
Risk-taking
Independence
Resourcefulness
Wholeheartedness
Initiative
Respect
Authenticity
Financial
Legacy
Simplicity
Balance
Forgiveness
Freedom
Love
Friendship
Loyalty
Stewardship
Belonging
Job security

Legacy
Simplicity
Balance
Forgiveness
Freedom
Love
Optimism
Time
Commitment
Grace
Order
Tradition
Community
Gratitude
Parenting
Compassion
Being a good husband
Being a healthy parent
Growth
Patience
Trust
Competence
Harmony
Truth
Confidence
Health
Peace
Understanding
Connection
Home
Perseverance
Contentment
Honesty
Contribution
Dignity
Vision
Cooperation
Humility
Pride
Vulnerability
Courage
Humor
Safety
Wealth
Creativity
Reliability
Curiosity

Characteristics or traits are qualities that describe your strengths and uniqueness. These reflect the nature of Jesus.

Accountable
Adaptable
Balanced
Blameless
Brother's Keeper
Bold
Brave
Charitable
Cleanliness
Commitment
Community-Oriented
Compassionate
Confident
Consistent
Content
Dependable
Determined
Devoted
Discerning
Disciplined
Driven
Ethical
Faithful
Focused
Forgiving
Friendly
Fun
Gentle
Giving
Godly
Goodness
Graceful
Gracious
Gratitude
Growth
Hard Working
Helpful
Honest
Honorable
Hopeful
Humble
Intelligent
Joyful
Just
Kind
Knowledgeable
Lawful

Leader
Listener
Loving
Loyal
Mature
Meek
Mindful
Motivating
Obedient
Organized
Patient
Peaceful
Polite
Positive
Prayerful
Pure
Real
Rejoicing
Reliable
Resourceful
Respectful
Responsible
Righteous
Secure
Self-Controlled
Self-Motivated
Server
Sharing
Sincere
Smart
Sociable
Spiritual
Stable
Steadfast
Steward
Structured
Submissive
Supportive
Sympathetic
Teachable
Team player
Thankful
Thoughtful
Trustworthy
Understanding
Wise
Zealous

LIVING LIKE CHRIST

Read each scripture then in the box write a simple sentence, summarizing what the scripture is teaching you. Use this worksheet to practice living your life with these same principles empowered by God to be a Difference Maker!

1
Psalm 71:8

2
Luke 4:8

3
Psalm 27:8

4
Psalm 29:2

5
Psalm 111:10

DEAR

METHUSELAH

Write a one-page letter to Methuselah sharing how his life inspires you. Share what you've learned from his example and how he's encouraged you to be a Difference Maker in your home, school and community.

LETTER TWO

ADAM

ADAM

SERVED THE COMMUNITY AS:

THE FIRST MAN TO BE FRUITFUL AND MULTIPLY

Strong Traits: Creative, Steward, Purposeful

Adam's name meaning in Hebrew: "Mankind," human," "man" and "Adamah" which means "ground"

Lesson: God was intentional when He created men. He wanted men to represent His image and likeness in the earth. God created men to not only produce fruit but to multiply for expansion. A righteous man uses his creativity to engage in purposeful work that doesn't just benefit himself but advances God's kingdom and increases worship of Him in the earth.

Write the definition of each word.

CREATIVE	STEWARD	PURPOSEFUL

Read Genesis 1:1-24. Notice God created the world by speaking into existence first what He wanted. Each day God created something new. After He spoke what He wanted, scripture follows up with the phrases, "And it was so" or "And God saw it was good" once God's work was completed. Scripture shows these three things were consistent when God created the heavens and the earth:

1. He said out loud what He wanted to create.
2. He spoke the purpose the created thing would serve.
3. What He made was good.

Read Genesis 1:26. This scripture outlines the creation of mankind within these three facts: 1) God spoke out loud what He wanted to create. 2) He spoke the purpose for bringing Adam into existence, and 3) He called making the man "good." Fill in the blanks.

Then God said, " Let us _________ ___________ in our own image, in our likeness, so ______ ______ _______ over the fish in the sea and the birds in the sky, ___________ the livestock and all the wild animals, and ________ _________ the creatures that move along the ground."

Read Genesis 1:27-28. Fill in the blanks for verse 28. These are three instructions God gave Adam. He also instructs you, as a man to:

"Be ______________ and _________________ in number.

Fill the ______________ and __________________ it.

______________ ____________ the fish in the sea and the birds in the sky and _______ ________ living creature that moves on the ground."

ADAM

SERVED THE COMMUNITY AS:

THE FIRST MAN TO BE FRUITFUL AND MULTIPLY

GOD PARTNERED WITH ADAM, GIVING HIM CREATIVE AUTHORITY.

Read Genesis 2:1-9 and 15-24.

In verse 15, where did God put Adam and why did He put Him there?

In verse 19-20, is the first time we read the man being creative. The LORD God could have named all the wild animals and birds, but He let Adam name them. The Bible says whatever Adam decided to call them "that was its name" (verse 19). Here we see God allowing Adam to exercise rulership over His creation. God partners with Adam to establish order on the earth. Adam had no book to study, no teacher to teach him so how was he intelligent enough to name all the animals?

Read and write in the space below Genesis 2:7.

Its God's Holy Spirit described as the "breath of life" breathed into Adam's nostrils that caused Him to become a "living being." When God formed Adam out of the dust of the ground He created Him in His image. When God spoke that Adam would be made in His likeness, this meant Adam would have wisdom and intelligence as God. The wisdom Adam had to name the animals and commune with God came from God speaking into existence Adam's life before He formed Him. In Genesis 1:26 God spoke that Adam would be made in "...Our image and in our likeness."

Son of God, the Bible instructs you to hold strongly to wisdom because it is through God's wisdom that you're able to live your life safely and do your work productively. Read Proverbs 3:19-24 and fill in the blanks:

"By __________ the LORD laid the earth's foundations, by ________________ He set the heavens in place; by _______ ______________ the watery depths were divided, and the clouds let drop the dew. My son, do not let wisdom and understanding out of your sight, preserve sound judgment and discretion; they will be __________ __________ _________, an ornament to grace your neck. Then you will go on your way in ____________, and your ___________ will not ______________. When you lie down, you will _________ be _______________; when you lie down, your sleep will be ____________.

AN IRONCLAD MAN IS...

CREATIVE. A STEWARD. PURPOSEFUL.

An ironclad man lives purposely to fulfill his Heavenly Father's command. He lives confidently knowing that he was made in the image and likeness of the Wise God. He does not shy away from his divine mandate "to be fruitful and multiply." Instead, he continually fellowships with the Holy Spirit of God, receiving divine instructions to manage the life God has given him. When an ironclad man receives his assignment from God, he speaks by faith then gets to work, doing the will of God. Filled with wisdom and the Holy Spirit, he creatively stewards the things God put Him in charge of. The ironclad man experiences growth, expansion and abundance because he has the favor of God on what he does, living a life of whatever he does "...he does it heartily, as to the LORD and not to men" (Colossians 3:23).

READ EACH VERSE. **WRITE THE SCRIPTURES IN THE BLANK SPACE.**

Creative

Proverbs 22:1 and 29

Steward

1 Peter 4:10-11

Purposeful

Psalm 57:2

Psalm 138:8

Read Exodus 35:30-35

Who did the LORD choose and fill with His Spirit?

What else does verse 31 say that God filled him with?

Psalm 24:1-2, "The earth is the LORD's, and everything in it, the world, and all who live in it; for He founded it on the seas and established it on the waters." God created the man to steward the earth He created. God created you, son of God to be a steward of your life, your family, your work, your schooling, your community. These things belong to God but He's given them to you as a gift to take care of. Depend on the LORD to help you be a faithful steward by being led by the Holy Spirit who gives you the power to walk in the truth, walk by faith and be successful in your life. Jesus says, "If you love me, you will keep my commandments. And I will ask the Father, and He will give you another Helper, to be with you forever, even the Spirit of truth, whom the world cannot receive, because it neither sees him nor knows him. You know him, for he dwells with you and will be in you" (John 14:15-17, ESV). The Holy Spirit gives you the power to help you fulfill God's command to you to be a steward of creation. Pray to God that He'll reveal His will to you on how He wants you to show up in your community and for your family so you can be fruitful and multiply in your life.

DISCUSSION QUESTIONS

These questions are designed for a deeper personal study or group discussion for ages 11 years old and up. If you're doing this study individually, write your answers.

Use your Notes page for extra writing space.
If you do this with a group discuss your answers.

Read Matthew 25:14-30. In this parable Jesus is talking about Himself as "the man" and the servants as "you." In Matthew 25:14-15, after the man called his servants, what did he entrust his servants with?

According to verse 15 how did the man determine how many bags of gold to give each servant?

Read 1 Peter 4:10-11 and Hebrews 13:20-21. What are the commonalities of these scriptures? Pay attentions to the words, "equip you and God provides."

Read 1 Corinthians 4:1-2. What are the <u>two things</u> these scriptures say people should regard you as?

Read Jeremiah 17:5-10. The LORD differentiates from a man that is "cursed" and a man that is "blesed."

In verse 10 the LORD says He's looks at the heart and will judge every man according to his "conduct." Read Psalm 119:9. Discuss or write how a "young man can keep his way pure" living in the world the way it is today.

In Matthew 25:19, we read that the master returned from his long journey. The Bible specifically says He, "returned and settled accounts with them." In other words, he returned to collect what he gave them. It was time for the servants to be accountable to their master for what he left to them.

Stewards are required to be faithful. Write and discuss things what would stop men from being faithful stewards.

Write and discuss things that can be done to encourage faithful stewardship over God's wealth.

The Bible warns against laziness, advising that men were created to work. In John 5:17, Jesus said to them, "My Father is always at His work to this very day, and I too am working." Read the following scriptures and discuss or study the consequences of not working at things that are productive: 2 Thessalonians 3:10; Proverbs 10:4; Proverbs 19:15; Proverbs 10:5.

This parable is about <u>stewardship</u>, <u>accountability</u>, using <u>divine gifts</u> and being <u>productive</u>. Discuss how godly men practice these areas in their life. Write your simplest answer to each below then commit to supporting each other in accomplishing these. If you did this individually, write a commitment to yourself and God on how you plan to practice these.

Stewardship-

Accountability-

Using divine gifts-

Productivity-

NOTES

PRAYING GOD'S WILL FOR YOUR LIFE

Read Matthew 6:33 and Jeremiah 29:11-13. Write your prayer, asking God to reveal His will for your life. If you know God's will, write a fervent prayer, praying for strength as you wait for Him to make good on His promises at the right time.

LIVING LIKE CHRIST

Read each scripture then in the box write a simple sentence, summarizing what the scripture is teaching you. Use this worksheet to practice living your life with these same principles empowered by God to be a Difference Maker!

1
Luke 2:49

2
Romans 12:2

3
Matthew 5:16

4
Proverbs 3:6

5
Colossians 1:10

DEAR

ADAM

Write a one-page letter to Adam sharing how his life inspires you. Share what you've learned from his example and how he's encouraged you to be a Difference Maker in your home, school and community.

LETTER THREE

JOSEPH

JOSEPH

SERVED THE COMMUNITY AS:

AN EXAMPLE FOR OVERCOMING TEMPTATION

Strong Traits: Honorable, Integrity, Respectful

Joseph's name meaning in Hebrew: "God shall add" or "Increase"

Lesson: When temptation presents itself, before he acts, a righteous man will remember two things: his neighbor and his God. He will flee from lust, refusing to partake in behaviors that cause harm to himself, cause him to sin against his neighbor and sin against God.

Write the definition of each word.

HONORABLE	INTEGRITY	RESPECTFUL

Read Genesis 39:1-23. In verse 1-4, we see Joseph purchased by Potiphar as a slave, but he got promoted, becoming more to Potiphar as his attendant.

What does verses 1-4 state the LORD gave Joseph? What did Potiphar see over Joseph's life?

Read Psalm 90:17. What happens when the favor of the LORD is on you?

In Genesis 39:6-10, Potiphar's wife and Joseph have their verbal exchange when she came onto him. What was Joseph's response in verse 9? Who did he consider would be impacted if he agreed to Potiphar's wife's request? He calls this behavior "wicked."

Read Colossians 3:5-11. List what this scripture says, "Put to death," "Get rid of" and "Put away."

Read Colossians 3:12-17. List what this scripture says, "Put on," and "Clothe yourself with."

AN IRONCLAD MAN IS...

HONORABLE. INTEGRITY. RESPECTFUL.

An ironclad man flees from youthful lusts. He doesn't go places where lust is welcomed. He doesn't hang out in places where sin is permissible. When presented with the opportunity to sin he examines his heart first. In his heart are the commands of God. These commands help him to reason why engaging in sin is wrong, how it would be devasting to his relationship with God and an injustice to his neighbor. He keeps the bigger picture of his destiny in the forefront of his mind and pursuits. A righteous man runs away fast, as fast as Joseph did from Potiphar's wife's lustful advances. He knows there's nothing but destruction for his soul that follows her sinful and spiritually deadly enticement.

READ EACH VERSE. **WRITE THE SCRIPTURES IN THE BLANK SPACE.**

Honorable

2 Corinthians 8:21

Romans 12:10

Integrity

Proverbs 11:3

Titus 2:7

Respectful

Matthew 7:12

Hebrews 12:9

Read Psalm 37. Write in the blank space verse 25.

This story of Potiphar's wife attempting to seduce Joseph then lying on him when he turned her down shows that sometimes doing the right thing can lead to persecution. Joseph refused to dishonor Potiphar and God by turning down Potiphar's wife's advances and still ended up in prison. Despite Joseph's imprisonment, in Genesis 39:20-21 while Joseph was in prison, "...the LORD was with him; He showed him kindness and granted favor in the eyes of the prison warden." Joseph ended up being in charge of the people who were held in prison. Although he lost the leadership position in Potiphar's house, God caused Joseph to recover that same position while in prison. I encourage you with this: when faced with the decision to make a moral decision that could cost you money, relationships or even your job, always know when you choose to please God, He'll never leave you alone to face the consequences of making the right decision. Be bold and stand for righteousness declaring just as King David did in Psalm 118:6, "The LORD is with me; I will not be afraid. What can mere mortals do to me?"

DISCUSSION QUESTIONS

These questions are designed for a deeper personal study or group discussion for ages 11 years old and up. If you're doing this study individually, write your answers.

Use your Notes page for extra writing space.
If you do this with a group discuss your answers.

Lust means to have an intense craving for something. Lust is often associated with sex, but someone can also lust for money, power, position, food or fame among other things. When you experience the world, you do so with your five senses: touch, taste, smell, sight, hearing. When one wants to control lustful behaviors, there are two important factors that one must remember in order to live life where they're not pursuing after lusts. One must be spiritually and physically aware (how they're engaging in the world through their five sense). In other words, one must have self-awareness and have discernment.

Do a web search then write the definitions. Discuss and/or write your answers on your notes page, how these help avoid falling into the temptation of lust.

Self-awareness:

Discernment:

Read 1 John 2:15-16. Discuss and/or write your answers on your notes page:

What is considered "the world" this scripture tells us not to love? (Read Matthew 6:24).
Define "the lust of the flesh." (Read 1 Peter 2:11-12 and Galatians 5:19-21).
Define "the lust of the eyes." (Read Genesis 3:6, Matthew 5:28 and Proverbs 6:25).
Define "the pride of life." (Read Proverbs 11:2, Proverbs 16:5, Proverbs 27:2 and Proverbs 29:23).

Read 2 Samuel Chapters 11 and 12. Discuss or answer the following questions on your notes page.
In chapter 11 verses 3-5, how did the "lust of the eyes" and "lust of the flesh" entrap David?

We discussed Joseph's ability to flee from Potiphar's wife's advances because he did two things: He respected his neighbor (Potiphar) and God, which were the reasons why he turned her down. David was just walking on his roof. There was nothing wrong with that. However, in chapter 11 verse 3-5, what steps did David take to dishonor God and Uriah when he acted on his lustful passions?

In chapter 12 verses 1-4 is the parable Samuel the prophet told David from the LORD to describe what he'd just done to Uriah. Notice in these verses the emphasis was placed on how David totally disregarded his neighbor, his brother in the LORD. How he took the little Uriah had although David had so much. Discuss how sin impacts others and the community. Why is it important to make the right decisions for the betterment of the community and brotherhood?

Read and write the scriptures. The following scripture to each tells you how to avoid lust.

Asks you how to stay pure:

Psalm 119:9

The answer to how to live according to God's word:

Psalm 119:10-11

NOTES

FORGIVING PEOPLE WHO'VE WRONGED YOU

If you've ever been hurt by someone who told lies on you, wronged you, rejected or abandoned you, this moment is for you to process your thoughts and feelings about this issue. This could be anyone such as a past or current relationship, a parent, a family member, friend or someone connected to your profession.
On the next page I encourage you to write a prayer of forgiveness, forgiving the person(s) who hurt or wronged you. I encourage you to forgive them so you can move on in the freedom of Christ. It's important to talk about your thoughts and emotions and not suppress them. Talking about your emotions and thought, about your pain and offense makes space for you to forgive, let go and move forward in wellness. If you need additional support, talk to a person you trust, a therapist or receive pastoral counseling.

If someone has hurt your feelings, rejected your friendship or bullied you, I pray that God heals your heart. On the next page I encourage you to write a prayer of forgiveness. Ask God to help you forgive them, to heal your emotions, and to bless them. If you need more support, ask a trusted adult to talk with you and pray with you.

PRAYER OF FORGIVENESS

LIVING LIKE CHRIST

Read each scripture then in the box write a simple sentence, summarizing what the scripture is teaching you. Use this worksheet to practice living your life with these same principles empowered by God to be a Difference Maker!

1
1 Thessalonians 4:3-5

2
1 Peter 2:17

3
Proverbs 4:25-27

4
Micah 6:8

5
Matthew 5:27-28

DEAR

JOSEPH

Write a one-page letter to Joseph sharing how his life inspires you. Share what you've learned from his example and how he's encouraged you to be a Difference Maker in your home, school and community.

LETTER FOUR

ZACCHAEUS

ZACCHAEUS

SERVED THE COMMUNITY AS:

EXAMPLE OF REPENTANCE

Strong Traits: Repentant, Lover of God, Seeker

Zacchaeus name meaning in Hebrew "Zakkai": "Pure" or "Clean"

Lesson: Jesus doesn't let sins stop Him from seeing the person. He looks past the actions and sees the person's need for Him. God wants a man that knows he needs Jesus and is willing to let him into his heart.

Write the definition of each word.

REPENTANT	**LOVER OF GOD**	**SEEKER**

Read Luke 19:1-9.
This story talks about Zacchaeus the chief tax collector for the Romans. The Bible says he was wealthy. The importance of knowing the financial status of Zacchaeus is because his wealth came from dishonest means. In Bible times, tax collectors were Jewish men who would collect more taxes from the Jews than they owed. Then they would pocket the extra money for profit.

Zacchaeus was a seeker. Read Luke 19:3-4. What did Zacchaeus do to see Jesus?

Jesus didn't allow Zacchaeus' current position as a tax collector stop him from calling Zacchaeus and going into his home. How do the people in verse 7 react to Jesus' seeing Zacchaeus?

When Zacchaeus experienced the acceptance of Jesus it lead to him repenting in verse 8.

What was Jesus' response to Zacchaeus in verse 9?

Who was saved because Zacchaeus repented?

Who did Jesus say He came to seek and to save?

AN IRONCLAD MAN IS...

REPENTANT. A LOVER OF GOD. A SEEKER.

An ironclad man is not perfect, but he seeks after Jesus. He sees the error of his ways, committing to the LORD to do right. Some people will know his past and when he makes mistakes. People will talk about those mistakes, but God will never turn him away when he comes to Him. Jesus' forgiveness and willingness to be with him despite who he is lead him to right his wrongs. No matter who's watching or what the naysayers say, an ironclad man is going to live for God because he loves Him. He chooses to live a life of repentance and worship. Overtime, he'll become strengthen to avoid temptation, stand strongly in his godly convictions and not compromise his faith.

READ EACH VERSE. **WRITE THE SCRIPTURES IN THE BLANK SPACE.**

Repentance

Matthew 3:8

Luke 5:32

Lover of God

1 John 4:19

Deuteronomy 6:5

Seeker

Deuteronomy 4:29

Matthew 6:33

Read Romans 6:23. Jesus suffered and died so you can live. He was beat with what's called a "cat of nine tails" or a "scourge." This whip had sharp objects at the end. This story doesn't end with Jesus' death. Read John chapters 19 and 20 to study Jesus' death, burial and resurrection.

Just like Zacchaeus, it doesn't matter what you've done. It doesn't matter who you are. And it doesn't matter what people say about you being a "sinner." The LORD sees you like He saw Zacchaeus in that tree. He wants to come into your heart, mind and soul and better your life.

Read Revelation 3:19-22.

DISCUSSION QUESTIONS

These questions are designed for a deeper personal study or group discussion for ages 11 years old and up. If you're doing this study individually, write your answers.

Use your Notes page for extra writing space.
If you do this with a group discuss your answers.

The Holy Trinity: God, Three in One. Read 2 Corinthians 13:14. There are three persons in One God. Read the scriptures and write in 3-5 words what it says about each person of God.

Grace of Jesus Christ-John 1:3

Love of God-1 Corinthians 8:6

Fellowship of the Holy Spirit-John 14:26

Salvation through Jesus Christ only. Read John 14:6 and John 3:16-21. What did God give the world because He loved it so much? Why (vs 16)? What did God not send Jesus into the world to do (vs 17)? What did God send Jesus into the world to do (vs 17)? Who is not condemned (vs 18)?

Born Again through the Holy Spirit. Read John 3:1-8. What does someone have to do to see the kingdom of God (vs 3)? There are two things a person must be born of to enter the kingdom of God. What are they (vs 5)? How does Jesus describe the Holy Spirit (vs 8)?

Living by God's Grace. Read Romans 8:1-14. What does the word condemnation mean? Why is there no condemnation (vs 1)? What did Christ condemn (vs 3)? What don't believers in Jesus live by (vs 4)? What do believers in Jesus live by (vs 5)?

NOTES

SALVATION THROUGH FAITH IN JESUS CHRIST

Jesus Loves You

Jesus wants to be a part of your life. He wants to bring His light, love, grace and guidance. However, He can't provide guidance, and He won't do this without your desire and invitation for Him to be the LORD and Savior of your life. If you do not have a relationship with Jesus or you've stopped living for God for some time, doing things your own way, this is an invitation for you to pray the prayer of salvation. You can pray this prayer by faith by yourself or with others. If you pray from your heart the LORD God can hear you and you'll be saved. Once you pray, you'll be born again and receive the Holy Spirit.

Eternal Life through Christ Jesus

"Jesus replied, "Very truly I tell you, no one can see the kingdom of God unless they are born again… no one can enter the kingdom of God unless they are born of water and the Spirit."
(John 3:3;5)

"Very truly I tell you, whoever hears my word and believes Him who sent me has eternal life and will not be judged but has crossed over from death to life."
(John 5:24)

Salvation comes through Confession and Belief

"If you declare with your mouth, "Jesus is LORD," and believe in your heart that God raised Him from the dead, you will be saved. For it is with your heart that you believe and are justified, and it is with your mouth that you profess your faith and are saved."
(Roman 10:9-10)

Prayer of Salvation

"Heavenly Father, I come to You as a sinner. I believe that Jesus Christ is Your Son, that He died for my sins, was buried and You raised Him from the dead three days later. I turn from my sins and accept Jesus as my LORD and Savior. Please forgive me and help me live a new life for You. In Jesus' Name, Amen."

You are saved!

What happens after you pray the prayer of salvation?

- Your name is written in the Book of Life (Revelation 3:5).
- Find a local Church to attend to grow into a disciple of Jesus Christ. This Church should believe in the Holy Trinity: The Father, Son and Holy Spirit and teach Jesus is the only way to God because of His death, burial and resurrection.
- Grow in your relationship with God the Father through Jesus Christ by reading the Bible so you can learn more about God. Reading the books of John and Acts is a good start to learn about God the Father, the Son and Holy Spirit.
- Pray every day in the "Name of Jesus." This is important because it is only through Jesus, we have access to God and power.
- Get baptized at your local Church.
- Join a small group for spiritual support and fellowship.
- Don't try to do the Christian walk alone. Join a body of believers.

OVERCOMING GENERATIONAL CURSES, SIN AND TRAGEDY

Tragedy strikes. Sin destroys. Generational curses keep boys and men in cycles of spiritual bondage. The Bible says, "It is for freedom that Christ has set us free. Stand firm, then, and do not let yourselves be burdened again by a yoke of slavery" (Galatians 5:1, NIV).
Use this sheet to list active areas in your life that aren't reflecting freedom. Find scriptures that support victory in these areas then pray to God to set you and your family free.

Christ is your peace, Jehovah Shalom. Seek peace from Him for grief, failures and rejection.

Examples of generational curses, sin or tragedy: poverty, gossiping, crime and incarceration, abuse, shame and guilt.

- Is there anything causing you to feel sad, mad, hurt, angry, disappointed, disgusted, or scared? You can write it here as a letter to God then read it to Him in prayer.

LIVING LIKE CHRIST

Read each scripture then in the box write a simple sentence, summarizing what the scripture is teaching you. Use this worksheet to practice living your life with these same principles empowered by God to be a Difference Maker!

1
Luke 18:9-14

2
Luke 18:18-29

3
Acts 3:19

4
Proverbs 8:17

5
Acts 17:30

DEAR

ZACCHAEUS

Write a one-page letter to Zacchaeus sharing how his life inspires you. Share what you've learned from his example and how he's encouraged you to be a Difference Maker in your home, school and community.

LETTER FIVE

JOHN THE BAPTIST

JOHN THE BAPTIST

SERVED THE COMMUNITY AS:

PROPHET AND PRIEST

Strong Traits: Devoted, Focused, Reliable

John's name meaning in Hebrew: "Yahweh is gracious."

Lesson: A man who knows his assignment is focused. He'll remain devoted to his calling until the end. When people bring confusing messages, he's reliable, staying true to the only message that matters: Jesus Christ is the Messiah.

Write the definition of each word.

DEVOTED	FOCUSED	RELIABLE

Read Luke 1:5-17; Luke 1:39-45; 57-80. Who is Zechariah? What was Zechariah's job?

Who is Elizabeth? Who is she a descendant of?

Read Number 3:5-13. Who did the LORD tell Moses to bring to Aaron? What does verses 7-8 say their responsibilities were?

Read Luke 1:6. How does the Bible describe Zechariah and Elizabeth?

Read Luke 1:76-79, Zechariah's song. Summarize what Zechariah's declares over his son's life. This sums up John's purpose, his assignment on earth. Hint: the word, "called," "you will go," and "to give."

AN IRONCLAD MAN IS...

DEVOTED. FOCUSED. RELIABLE.

An ironclad man is pre-destined for greatness. Before he comes into the world there is an assignment on his life. He is a son of the Most High before he is anything to anyone. As he grows in the wisdom and strength of the LORD, he remains close to his Heavenly Father, not being afraid to stand out. He's not afraid to be different. He's not afraid to stand up for righteousness even if it leaves him standing alone. He doesn't seek the approval of man, but lives his life devoted to the call of his Father. Willing to go the road less traveled, he becomes less to make the Name of Jesus greater in the earth.

READ EACH VERSE. **WRITE THE SCRIPTURES IN THE BLANK SPACE.**

Devoted

Galatians 2:20

Focused

Proverbs 16:3

Colossians 3:2

Reliable

Hebrews 10:23

Proverbs 11:3

Read John 3:25-30.
Write verse 30.

Self-reflect: As believers we're called to live a life that glorifies God. Think of an area(s) of your life that can "become less" and Christ can "become greater." Write it in the blank then say a prayer, asking God to help you bring glory to Him in this area.

DISCUSSION QUESTIONS

These questions are designed for a deeper personal study or group discussion for ages 11 years old and up. If you're doing this study individually, write your answers.

Use your Notes page for extra writing space.

John is called, "John the Baptist." This signifies the role he played in God establishing the New Covenant with His people. John's job was to prepare the way for Jesus. He also was baptizing people who repented for their sins. Read Luke 3:1-18. In verse 16 what does John say he baptizes with?

What are the two things John said Jesus will baptize with?

Read Matthew 3:13-17. In verse 15 why did Jesus say it was important to be baptized?

Who descended on Jesus?

Read Acts 1:1-8. In verse 8 what does Jesus say the Holy Spirit gives to the believer once He comes upon them?

The Holy Spirit empowers the believer to do what?

Read John 3:1-21. Jesus says flesh gives birth to flesh and the Spirit gives birth to the spirit. In verse 21, He also says that "...whoever lives by the truth comes into the light so that it may be seen plainly that what they have done has been done in the sight of God."

Read Galatians 5:19-21, Romans 8:8, James 4:7 and Proverbs 22:3-6. Discuss with your group how boys and men can identify the behaviors of the flesh and the ideas or trends in the world they're connected to. Discuss how to avoid them to walk with God.

John faithfully fulfilled his assignment. When Jesus was ready to start his ministry; John was in position for Jesus to be baptized. Jesus had to be baptized to "fulfill all righteousness" so He could enter the next phase of His ministry as water baptism is a part of the New Covenant. In John 3:1-21 we read Jesus met Nicodemus, sharing the New Covenant with him for salvation. Then the Samaritan woman in John 4, sharing with her the truth of a "Living Water" who could quench her thirst. These people were touched by Jesus as a result of John surrending his life to God's will which was to prepare the way for Jesus.
God has a calling on your life to serve His people in the Church or in the world or both. There are people who are waiting to experience God through your testimony. Pray God will show you your assignment and build you up in His righteousness. If you know your assignment, I encourage you to seek God for ways to share Jesus with others. If you're already working in your assignment may God bless, strengthen, provide for and keep you.

NOTES

You are a Messenger of Jesus Christ

You are God's son, His messenger. Like John the Baptist, Jesus commissioned you to tell people that He is the Messiah, to lead people to repentance, baptizing them in the Name of the Father, the Son and the Holy Spirit.

As a believer you've been called to be baptized by water and the Holy Spirit. Water is the santification of sins. The Holy Spirit is the power of God who transforms you into the image of Christ to do the will of God.

If you're saved and have confessed Jesus as your Savior but are not baptized, I encourage you to go to your pastor or find a church to be baptized as this is an important step for "fulfilling all righteousness."

Read Matthew 28: 16-20. Summarize Jesus' last words to believers.

Read Romans 10:9-10. What does Paul say about confession?

Read Romans 6:23. What is the gift of God?

Based off what you've just learned, take this information and write a 5-10 sentence (1-2 paragraphs) of how you would share Jesus with a non-believer. Make sure your statement is based on the scriptures you just learned. Keep it simple. When you have an opportunity, share this statement with someone you know needs Jesus as their personal LORD and Savior, encouraging them to be baptized in water.

LIVING LIKE CHRIST

Read each scripture then in the box write a simple sentence, summarizing what the scripture is teaching you. Use this worksheet to practice living your life with these same principles empowered by God to be a Difference Maker!

1
Acts 22:16

2
2 Corinthians 5:17

3
John 1:29

4
Romans 6:3-4

5
Romans 10:14

DEAR

JOHN THE BAPTIST

Write a one-page letter to John the Baptist sharing how his life inspires you. Share what you've learned from his example and how he's encouraged you to be a Difference Maker in your home, school and community.

LETTER SIX

KING DAVID

KING DAVID

SERVED THE COMMUNITY AS:

A GOOD FRIEND

Strong Traits: Tenderhearted, Loyal, Kind

King David's name meaning in Hebrew:
"Beloved" and "Uncle"

Lesson: Being filled with the Holy Spirit makes a righteous man a whole, well-rounded person. He's emotionally intelligent, honors others and values his relationships. Because he's filled with kindness, love and a giving heart, God can bless him with much because He knows that his son will use the abundance given to him to enrich the lives of others.

Write the definition of each word.

TENDERHEARTED **LOYAL** **KIND**

Read about Jonathan and David's friendship in 1 Samuel 18:1-4. In your own words, describe the friendship of David and Jonathan.

Read 1 Samuel 18:5-8 which talks about how much Saul despised David although he did nothing wrong to Saul. Despite of Saul, Jonathan's father hating David, Jonathan and David remained loyal to each other because they both let the love of their friendship be stronger than hate. 1 Corinthians 13:1-13 indicates what true love is. Turn to page 54 to complete the assignment on "Loving like God."

Read 2 Samuel 9:1-13. Verses 1 and 3 reveal David's intentions to show kindness to anyone in the house of Saul. What was the name of the person left in Saul's house? What does verses 7-10 say Saul's grandson, Jonathan's son was left?

LOVING LIKE GOD

Read 1 Corinthians 13:1-13. Make a list of what this scripture says love is then commit to practice this with others every day.

AN IRONCLAD MAN IS...

TENDERHEARTED. LOYAL. KIND.

An ironclad man is a good friend. He is strong and brave when the time calls for it. He's also tenderhearted, loyal and kind in his relationships. He values the love and care of a good friend. He values his relationships, looking for ways to honor his friends and show kindness. He provides support where it is needed. He remains loyal even when others aren't loyal to him, being a friend whose love "covers a multitude of sins" (1 Peter 4:8). The fruits of the Holy Spirit are on full display in his life, bringing glory to God his Heavenly Father.

READ EACH VERSE. **WRITE THE SCRIPTURES IN THE BLANK SPACE.**

Tenderhearted

Ephesians 4:32

Loyal

Proverbs 17:17

Kind

Luke 6:35

Read Proverbs 11:17. What is this scripture saying?

Read Galatians 5:19-21.
Think back to Saul's behavior towards David. What acts of the flesh do you recognize in Saul's behavior specifically in 1 Samuel 18:5-8.
What does the Bible warn about people who pracitce these behaviors?

DISCUSSION QUESTIONS

These questions are designed for a deeper personal study or group discussion for ages 11 years old and up. If you're doing this study individually, write your answers.

Use your Notes page for extra writing space.

In Galatians 5, God declares freedom and life are experienced when we walk in step with the Spirit. How do you know you're walking in step with the Spirit? Read page 57, the fruits of the Spirit, to understand what walking in step with the Spirit of God is. This is a chance for you to do a personal reflection on the areas you are strong in and the areas that are in need of improvement. Below list the fruits of the Spirit you display then make a list of fruits you're going to commit to praying the LORD will help you increase in your life. Then practice those.

Fruits of the Spirit I'm Strong at Showing to Others	Fruits of the Spirit I'm Committing to Praying that God will Increase in Me

Read Galatians 5:13-18. The Bible says, "If you bite and devour each other, watch out or you will be destroyed by each other" (verse 15). This happens when we don't practice the fruits of the Spirit. Are there relationships in your life that need God's healing touch? If so, list those relationships here and commit to praying for those people and those relationships. Pray God's will be accomplished for you and those people pertaining to your relationship with them. Pray God will increase the fruits of His Spirit in your relationships.

Read 2 Samuel 1:1-27. Although Saul tried to take David's life, he still remained tenderhearted and honored the seat Saul sat in as king. He felt grief for Saul's death, speaking kindly of him and his friend Jonathan in verse 23. It's not always easy to love your enemies and remain friendly and kind to someone who hates you, but Jesus says, "But I tell you, love your enemies. Pray for those who persecute you that you may be children of your Father in heaven" (Matthew 5:44-45).

If you are finding it difficult to love people especially your enemies, pray God will help you with this. Pray that He'll increase your ability to display the fruits of the Holy Spirit. Pray for a kind, loyal and tender heart like David's.

FRUITS OF

THE SPIRIT

Below is the fruits of the Holy Spirit and the meaning of each word. Notice "love" is in the center. If you focus on loving others the rest of the fruits will be a result of love, for you can't be kind, patient, gentle. etc., without being loving. Read Galatians 5:22-23 and become familiar with these and practice each one in your daily life.

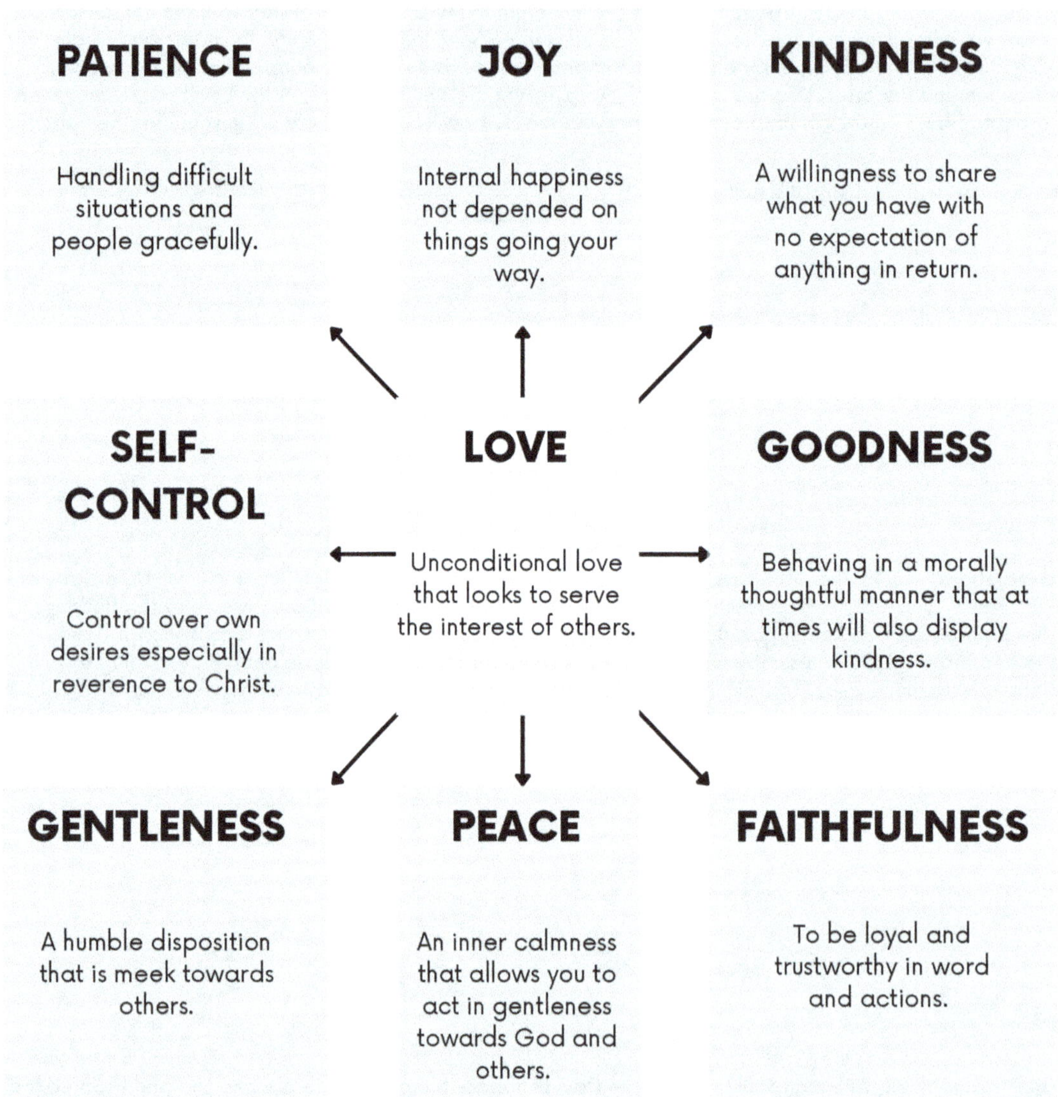

"You, my brothers and sisters, were called to be free. But do not use your freedom to indulge the flesh; rather, serve one another humbly in love. For the entire law is fulfilled in keeping this one command: "Love your neighbor as yourself." If you bite and devour each other, watch out or you will be destroyed by each other.
So I say, walk by the Spirit, and you will not gratify the desires of the flesh. For the flesh desires what is contrary to the Spirit, and the Spirit what is contrary to the flesh. They are in conflict with each other, so that you are not to do whatever you want. But if you are led by the Spirit, you are not under the law."

Galatians 5:13-18

NOTES

LIVING LIKE CHRIST

Read each scripture then in the box write a simple sentence, summarizing what the scripture is teaching you. Use this worksheet to practice living your life with these same principles empowered by God to be a Difference Maker!

1
Proverbs 21:21

2
John 15:13

3
1 Corinthians 13:7

4
Proverbs 20:6

5
Job 6:14

DEAR

KING DAVID

Write a one-page letter to King David sharing how his life inspires you. Share what you've learned from his example and how he's encouraged you to be a Difference Maker in your home, school and community.

LETTER SEVEN

BOAZ

BOAZ

SERVED THE COMMUNITY AS:

A KINSMAN-REDEEMER

Strong Traits: Supportive, Admirable, Considerate

Boaz's name meaning in Hebrew: "Strength"

Lesson: In life we face tragedies like Naomi and Ruth did when they lost everything they had and everyone, they loved. However, like Ecclesiastes 7:8 says, "The end of a matter is better than its beginning, and patience is better than pride." When a man humbles himself before Christ and allows Him to redeem him, God will restore everything he's lost, and no weapon formed against that man will be able to prosper.

Write the definition of each word.

SUPPORTIVE	ADMIRABLE	CONSIDERATE

Read the book of Ruth. In Ruth 2:20, Naomi praised God for Boaz. She was grateful that Boaz was kind to her and her deceased family members by being kind to Ruth. In verse 20 she says, "That man is our close relative; he is one of our guardian-redeemers." Another name for a guardian-redeemer is a "kinsman-redeemer." Read the following scriptures aboout God's commands for a kinsman-redeemer and the laws about redemption.

Read and write Leviticus 25:25.

Read Leviticus 25:47-49. In verse 49, who was able to redeem the Israelite after they were sold?

Read Romans 7:23. Who was Paul saying we are a "prisoner" to?

Read Romans 6:23. What is the penalty for sin?

Read Galatian 4:4-5. Why did God send Jesus?

Read and write Isaiah 47:4 about Christ our Reedemer.

AN IRONCLAD MAN IS...

SUPPORTIVE. ADMIRABLE. CONSIDERATE.

An ironclad man stands in the gap for his family and community when lack and loss present themselves. He positions himself steady and ready financially, mentally, physically and spiritually to rise up to the occasion when God is in need of a righteous man to intercede or be a resource to bless His people who are in need. A righteous man is an upstanding man, those who know him describe him as admirable. He considers others before himself. His heart and mind are positioned to support the cause of God and that is to "Defend the weak and the fatherless; uphold the cause of the poor and oppressed" (Psalm 82:3).

READ EACH VERSE. **WRITE THE SCRIPTURES IN THE BLANK SPACE.**

Supportive

Acts 20:35

Admirable

Proverbs 22:1

Considerate

Philippians 2:4

1 Corinthians 10:24

Read and write
1 Timothy 2:5-6

Read Matthew 1:1-17, the Genealogy of Jesus the Messiah. Write verses 5 and 6.
Notice Boaz, the kinsman-redeemer in the bloodline that leads to the birth of great men like King David and King Solomon. This bloodline includes King Jesus, the ultimate Kinsman-Redeemer, the relative from this bloodline who redeemed His people, the Israelites and the entire world from slavery to sin by paying the price of sin which was death with His life.

DISCUSSION QUESTIONS

These questions are designed for a deeper personal study or group discussion for ages 11 years old and up. If you're doing this study individually, write your answers.

Use your Notes page for extra writing space.

Boaz and Ruth's marriage was symbolic for how Christ would redeem the Church. This story represents how Christ redeemed a people who were rejected and lost because of sin by paying a price (His life) to buy them back from death, hell and the grave.

Read Titus 2:11-14. What are we to say "No" to?

What did Christ redeem us from in verse 14? What did he purify us for?

Read Titus 2:6-8. In verse 6, what does this scripture say to "urge the young men" to do? Fill in the blanks.

To be________________________

Set ______________ an ________________ by doing what is ______________

In your teaching____

Titus 2:13 states that we're waiting for the appearance of the "glory of our great God and Savior Jesus Christ." The Bible talks about the second coming of Christ. Read the following scriptures and discuss or meditate on the instructions these scriptures are giving to believers about Christ coming back.

Matthew 24; 2 Peter 3:10; Revelation 22:12.

Read John 3:16 and Matthew 9:36.

The story of Ruth and Boaz represents a story of redemption. Boaz was willing to step in and redeem Ruth from widowhood, poverty and childlessness after the loss of her husband, brother and her father-in-law. These things she could not save herself from.

Humanity is like Ruth in this story. We were lost because of sin and had no way or no one to save us but Christ stepped in.

Jesus was both God and man who lived with a mission. He did not get distracted from His mission telling those who questioned his actions, "Why did you seek Me? Did you not know that I must be about My Father's business?" (Luke 2:49). He was God, seeing people suffer without a shepherd. He became the Kinsman-Redeemer for His people; the mediator who stepped in to fill in the gap that separated humanity from its Creator. He paid the price we owed for sin which was death.

He who knew no sin became sin so that you and I could live. The chastisement of our peace is on Him and by His stripes we are healed (Isaiah 53:5). He died on our behalf and now we have eternal life!

Give thanks to God for Jesus Christ our Savior forever! Remain in an attitude of gratitude that Jesus was willing to give Himself for a people who could not pay themselves. Worship and praise the LORD every day and every chance you get.

NOTES

LIVING LIKE CHRIST

Read each scripture then in the box write a simple sentence, summarizing what the scripture is teaching you. Use this worksheet to practice living your life with these same principles empowered by God to be a Difference Maker!

1
1 Corinthians 16:14

2
Hosea 2:19

3
Song of Solomon 4:9

4
Ephesians 5:2

5
Ephesians 5:25

DEAR

BOAZ

Write a one-page letter to Boaz sharing how his life inspires you. Share what you've learned from his example and how he's encouraged you to be a Difference Maker in your home, school and community.

LETTER EIGHT

AQUILA

AQUILA

SERVED THE COMMUNITY AS:

AN EXAMPLE OF A HUSBAND IN MINISTRY WITH HIS WIFE

Strong Traits: Hospitable, Teacher, Trailblazer

Aquila's name meaning in Latin: "Eagle."

Lesson: A man devoted to his God teams up with the helpmate God has given him, his wife, to fulfill the command of the Great Commission given to Christ-followers by Christ Himself. He and his wife together, go into the world and make disciples. When disciples are made, those disciples go and make more disciples.

Write the definition of each word.

HOSPITABLE	**TEACHER**	**TRAILBLAZER**

Read Acts 18.
We read that Aquila met Paul and he and his wife Priscilla took Paul in and started supporting him in his work as a tentmaker and his work preaching the Gospel.

From there in verse 18, it says Prisicilla and Aquila joined Paul from Corinth to Syria. They arrived in Ephesus in verse 19. Paul left them to go about his work, preaching and teaching about Jesus in the synagogue. Meanwhile, Aquila and Priscilla heard a man named "Apollos" preaching about Jesus.

How does verse 26 say Aquila and Priscilla served Apollos? What did they do for him?

What does verse 27-28 say Apollos did after his time with Aquila and Priscilla?

Read Romans 16:3, 1 Corinthians 16:19 and 2 Timothy 4:19. These are the greetings Paul continued to send to Aquila and Prisicilla as they continued to faithfully serve the LORD and His church. Notice in the greetings to the married couple, Paul also greets the church that met in their house. Not only did Aquila and Priscilla devote their time to traveling to support Paul, but they also taught about Jesus and were hospitable, opening up their house so their brothers and sisters in Christ could meet for church. Aquila and Priscilla are an example of a married couple who had their work as tentmakers to support their family, but they also devoted themselves to the work of the ministry of Jesus Christ.

AN IRONCLAD MAN IS...

HOSPITABLE. A TEACHER. A TRAILBLAZER.

An ironclad man uses his time and talent for God. He dedicates his life to be a light of Christ in his community and the world, giving and teaching others about Christ. He's a trailblazer because God uses him to pave the path for others to come to faith in Christ. An ironclad man doesn't work alone. He and his wife are God's dynamic duo! Together, living intentionally, he and his wife build up the Body of Christ. Willing to use their own resources, their focus is to partake in the ultimate goal: to preach so that God's children can hear and receive the redemption power of Jesus Christ. A righteous man lives to make disciples in Christ, teaching them to grow in the understanding and knowledge of their Creator.

READ EACH VERSE. **WRITE THE SCRIPTURES IN THE BLANK SPACE.**

Hospitable

Hebrews 13:16

Isaiah 58:7

Teacher

Luke 6:40

1 Timothy 4:13

Trailblazer

Leviticus 20:26

Being married or "equally yoked" with a wife that believes in Christ is a command from God in scripture.
Read 2 Corinthian 6:14-18.
Summarize why God commands this?

Self-reflect: Read Genesis 2:18, 1 Timothy 3:2; Ecclesiastes 4:9, Ecclesiates 9:9. These scriptures talk about the blessings and benefits of having a wife. Think about creative ways you and your wife or future wife can glorify God. In other words, if there were no limits, what can you see yourself doing? How could your wife help you?

DISCUSSION QUESTIONS

These questions are designed for a deeper personal study or group discussion for ages 11 years old and up. If you're doing this study individually, write your answers.

Use your Notes page for extra writing space.

Some people are called to full-time ministry. This would be people who work in the church as missionaries, pastors, administrators, bookkeepers, worship directors etc. There are some people who work part-time. Then there are people who volunteer serving in their church in different positions every week, such as deacons, ushers, child-care teachers, students volunteers, parking lot attendants, greeters, sound and media technicians, musicians, those who help lead worship or sing in the choir.
Everyone's called to serve the church in some capacity based on their gifts, talents, skills, abilities and calling. No matter if you work in the church fulltime, part-time or volunteer or are working in the community to support yourself, we're all called to share the Gospel of Jesus Christ in our communities and make disciples.

The Bible tells us to stir up the gifts! Some versions say to "fan into flame the gift of God" (2 Timothy 1:6, NIV). God is challenging you to dig deep, identify and use the gifts He's given you. Many people wonder what their gifts are. Think of what your passions, interests and hobbies are. What do you find joy in doing? When you see a problem in the world, do you feel compassionate about it or want to act? Do you find yourself planning or attempting to solve a problem? These natural desires could be an indication of how God has gifted you. There are also spiritual gifts, too. If it's a natural talent or a spiritual gift it should be used to serve God and others. We'll talk more about identifying your giftings in the Difference Maker section.

Read the following scriptures and write the spiritual gifts and offices Jesus established in the Church. Only write each gift one time as the same gift will appear in multiple scriptures. Romans 12:6-8; 1 Corinthians 12:4-11; Ephesians 4:11-13.

Read 1 Peter 4:10-11 and James 1:17. What should you use your gifts to do? Where do good and perfect gifts come from?

STIR UP YOUR GIFTS!
God may have called you to business, pastoring, government, teaching, public safety, public speaking, entertainment, architecture, science and so much more! Whatever you do and wherever you do it do it for the LORD!

NOTES

LIVING LIKE CHRIST

Read each scripture then in the box write a simple sentence, summarizing what the scripture is teaching you. Use this worksheet to practice living your life with these same principles empowered by God to be a Difference Maker!

1
James 5:16

2
Hebrews 13:7

3
Ephesians 5:19

4
1 John 2:10

5
1 Corithians 12:13

DEAR

AQUILA

Write a one-page letter to Aquila sharing how his life inspires you. Share what you've learned from his example and how he's encouraged you to be a Difference Maker in your home, school and community.

LETTER NINE

MOSES

MOSES

SERVED THE COMMUNITY AS:

PROPHET
LAWGIVER
MEDIATOR

Strong Traits: Tenacious, Merciful, Leadership

Moses' name meaning in Hebrew: "To draw out."

Lesson: A God-led leader understands God's assignment and wants to see it fulfilled. He doesn't have an ulterior motive. He sees to it that God's plan is carried out. Even through difficult times, he remains a tenacious, faithful and steadfast man under God's leadership.

Write the definition of each word.

TENACIOUS	MERCIFUL	LEADERSHIP

Read Exodus 17:8-16.

Who were Moses and the Israelites fighting against?

What were the orders Moses gave to Joshua?

In verse 9, what role did Moses say he was going to play in the battle?

During the battle, what happened when Moses' arms remained raised to God? What happened when his arms fell?

In verse 15, what did Moses do once the battle was over? How did he acknowledge God for their victory over their enemies?

Read Exodus 32. See in verse 11-14 how Moses interceded for mercy on behalf of the Israelites. Although he could've been made into a great nation, he chose to plead for mercy.

AN IRONCLAD MAN IS...

TENACIOUS. MERCIFUL. LEADERSHIP.

An ironclad man is a God-led leader that prays on behalf of others. He extends mercy and prays for God to have mercy on others. There's nothing he does such as being successful in school, playing sports, raising a family, leading a church or group, or working in the community without depending on God. A righteous man is strong. He boldly and humbly leads in the leadership position God's given him. He spends time in prayer and seeking the face of God for what to do next because he knows this is true: God is wisdom. Wisdom, good judgment and wise counsel only come from the Spirit of God. He seeks the LORD's face in prayer because he knows this is the only way he'll be successful.

READ EACH VERSE. **WRITE THE SCRIPTURES IN THE BLANK SPACE.**

Tenacious

Joshua 1:9

Philippians 4:13

Merciful

Luke 6:36

James 2:13

Leadership

1 Timothy 4:12

Matthew 7:12

A good leader uses wisdom and good judgment to make decisions. Read Proverbs 2:6-8 and Psalm 32:8-9. Summarize in your own words what these scriptures are teaching you about wisdom.

Self-reflect: Now that you've studied tenacity, leadership and mercy, think of how God would want you to use strength, leadership and mercy in your next challenge. How would you use these in conflict with someone? How would you use these to make a decision or give advice (help) to someone? Where would you search for the answer?

DISCUSSION QUESTIONS

These questions are designed for a deeper personal study or group discussion for ages 11 years old and up. If you're doing this study individually, write your answers.

Use your Notes page for extra writing space.

Read Exodus 19:1-9. Here we see Moses acting as a mediator between God and the Israelites. God told Moses what to say and Moses went back to the people to deliver God's message. As leaders, God does not send you into a leadership position alone. Like Moses, God knows how important it is for people to know that He's with you.

What does God say to Moses in verse 9 that he was going to do so the people would trust Moses?

God calls leaders to do one thing: Lead people to Himself so they can worship Him. Read Exodus 5:1; 7:16; 8:1; 9:1. During the Exodus when God was delivering His people from the bondage of Egypt, He sent Moses to tell Pharoah four different times to let the Israelites go so they can worship Him in the wilderness. As a leader, your responsibility is to encourage people to know and worship their Creator. In whatever capacity you are given to lead or bring God glory, people should hear about God and be encouraged to believe in and worship Him.

Read Revelation 12:11. Write the three key parts of the Christian faith that are important to being victorious as a son of God:

1)

2)

3)

Worshipping God is important to the believer's life, success and consistent connection with God. Read Exodus 26:30-37, about the first Tabernacle built so the people could worship God. These verses talk about the "Holy Place" and the "Most Holy Place." There was a curtain that separated the people from God's Spirit. Only once a year and only the high priest could enter the Most Holy Place, but he couldn't go without taking blood to offer for his sins and the sins of the people. What people needed was to be filled with the Holy Spirit, but we were separated from God because of sin. The visual separation was the curtain or veil that separated humanity from God.
Read Hebrews 9. Write verse 15 that indicates that Christ is our Mediator of the New Covenant.

Now that Christ has died and rose again, we're able to have the Spirit of God inside our hearts, souls, and minds. We now have a fulltime connection with God, atonement for sins and victory. Our bodies have become the new tabernacle for the Holy Spirit, replacing the earthly tabernacle. Read 1 Corinthians 6:19-20. We are called to honor God with our bodies because this is where He dwells now.

Read John 4. Then write verses 23-24.

DISCUSSION QUESTIONS

These questions are designed for a deeper personal study or group discussion for ages 14 years old and up. If you're doing this study individually, write your answers.

Use your Notes page for extra writing space.

Read Hebrews 12:18-28. Compare and contrast the Mountain of Fear and the Mountain of Joy.
How does the description of the Mountain of Joy reflect the relationship God wants to have with you?

Discuss the difference between "fearing the LORD" and being afraid of the LORD.
Read and discuss 2 Timothy 1:7-10. Write 2 Timothy 1:7.

In order to worship God properly, we must know who and who **not** to worship, how to live and how **not** to live.
Read Matthew 6:24 fill in the blanks.
"

_________ ____________ can serve two masters. Either you will ________ the one and _______ the other, or you will be _____________ to the one and ______________ the other. You ___________ serve both ________ and ___________."

Read Exodus 20:1-23 and Mark 12:28-31. Write Mark 12:30-31. According to Jesus, this sums up all the commandments. These two scriptures should guide your heart in worship and how you live.

Paul tells us how we "...ought to conduct ourselves in God's household, which is the Church of the living God, the pillar and foundation of truth" (1 Timothy 3:14-15, NIV).

Read 1 Timothy 4:1-15 to answer the following questions:
1) Verse 4:1-7-Today there are New Age teachings and "godless myths and old wives tales" (vs. 7) that abandon the truth that Jesus is the only Way, the Truth and Life. His death, burial and resurrection is minimized or not believed. Name at least one New Age teaching. Do you recognize them so you can deny these false teachings if they were presented to you? What does verse 6 say you should do?

2) 1 Timothy 4:7 says, "...train yourself to be godly." God created you multi-faceted meaning you have a mind, body, spirit and heart (thoughts and emotions which influence what you do). Search and write one scripture for each to learn how to reflect godliness. Use a web search engine for help to find scriptures.

Mind

Heart

Body

Spirit

NOTES

LIVING LIKE CHRIST

Read each scripture then in the box write a simple sentence, summarizing what the scripture is teaching you. Use this worksheet to practice living your life with these same principles empowered by God to be a Difference Maker!

1
Galatian 5:13

2
Luke 4:8

3
Psalm 95:6

4
Psalm 100:1-5

5
Philippians 2:3

DEAR

MOSES

Write a one-page letter to Moses sharing how his life inspires you. Share what you've learned from his example and how he's encouraged you to be a Difference Maker in your home, school and community.

LETTER TEN

ELIJAH

ELIJAH

SERVED THE COMMUNITY AS:

A WITNESS THAT GOD IS OUR SOURCE

Strong Traits: Faith, Bold, Confident

Elijah's name meaning in Hebrew: "Yahweh is my God."

Lesson: A man of faith puts his faith into action. He knows that "...faith by itself, if not accompanied by action, is dead" (James 2:17). He believes God can **be all he needs** (love, joy, peace and hope) and **will supply all his needs** (material and financial). When God instructs Him, he obeys. He's confident God will shows up to do the miraculous because God is his Source, fulfilling His promise to supply everything he needs.

Write the definition of each word.

FAITH **BOLD** **CONFIDENT**

Read 1 Kings 17:1-24. We read about three miracles. All miracles were directed at the instruction of the LORD God to Elijah. Elijah confidently obeyed the word of the LORD. The first miracle was to be no rain for a few years except at Elijah's word. The second was Elijah being fed by ravens. The third one was Elijah being fed by a widow who did not have enough. She was about to eat the last that she had and her and her son were about to die from poverty and starvation.

Notice in verse 13 Elijah requested the woman to bake the bread then bring it to him first. By obeying that instruction there was a promise attached to her obedience in verse 14. What did the LORD promise?

Read Leviticus 27:30 and Malachi 3:8-10. What does the LORD instruct about giving to Him first?

Read Proverbs 3:9-10 and Luke 6:38. What does the LORD promise will happen when we give?

Read Psalm 37:25. What does this passage tell you about God's provision to the righteous?

AN IRONCLAD MAN IS...

FAITH. BOLD. CONFIDENT.

An ironclad man knows where his help comes from his "...help comes from the LORD" (Psalm 121:1-2). Like Elijah, a godly man seeks the LORD's provision and wisdom regarding his life, children, family and his community. He's confident because he trusts the LORD, the Maker of heaven and earth whose hand is not too short to provide for His own. He walks by faith, boldly and wisely following instructions. Jehovah Jireh provides everything he needs plus more! Go to God and pray for what you need! The LORD will take care of you!

READ EACH VERSE. **WRITE THE SCRIPTURES IN THE BLANK SPACE.**

Faith

Luke 1:37

1 Corinthians 2:5

Bold

Proverbs 28:1

Ephesians 3:12

Confident

Philippians 1:6

Read Psalm 121:1-8. Meditate on the promises in this passage and summarize them. Write what God is promising you. Return and read this when you are in need. Pray on this. Meditate on this. Have faith because the LORD is with you.

Elijah experienced miracle after miracle! The LORD's provision for Elijah never stopped. When Elijah heard the instructions from the LORD, he received those words confidently, experiencing God's promise for provision. The widow in this passage obeyed the instructions of Elijah and was provided for as well. They both had enough food to make it through the famine because of their obedience. God will not just give you what you need but He'll always give MORE than enough. Read Ephesians 3:20 and walk by faith!

DISCUSSION QUESTIONS

These questions are designed for a deeper personal study or group discussion for ages 11 years old and up.

Use your Notes page for extra writing space.

Read and write Psalm 68:5. This scripture tells us that God protects and provides the needs of His people. These discussion questions will cover another miracle God performs for a widow and her sons through the prophet Elisha, Elijah's disciple, servant and successor (he came next) after God took Elijah from the earth (2 Kings 2:11).

Read 2 Kings 4:1-7. The Widow with the Olive Oil's husband passed away changing her status from wife to widow. In verse 1 what company was her husband a part of when he was alive?

Notice Elisha's answer in 2 Kings 4:2. He did not send her away but he asked how he could help her. Elisha was a prophet of the Most High God. You and I are the Church who represents the LORD. We have access to everything we need because He is our Source. God asks us to not send people away. Instead, provide what they need or seek the LORD for an answer. What did Elisha tell the widow to do with what she had?

In 2 Kings 4:6 when did the oil stop flowing?

In 2 Kings 4:7, what did Elisha tell the widow to do when she returned to him?

GOD WILL PROVIDE FOR YOU

Read the following scriptures. In the "God will provide" section, write 1-2 words summing up what this scripture says God will provide for you.

Psalm 91:1-16

God will provide ________________________________

Matthew 6:25

God will provide ________________________________

Psalm 34:17

God will provide ________________________________

James 5:16

God will provide ________________________________

NOTES

WHAT DO YOU NEED FROM THE LORD?

Write a list of things you need from God. For each need, find scripture, writing it next to the need. If you need help, use a search engine to look for scriptures by typing in "scripture on (insert need)." I encourage you to then open your physical Bible, find the scripture there, read it and then write it down here. Use this as a guide to pray for your needs with the scripture you wrote. Give everything to the LORD, waiting in faith for the miraculous!

LIVING LIKE CHRIST

Read each scripture then in the box write a simple sentence, summarizing what the scripture is teaching you. Use this worksheet to practice living your life with these same principles empowered by God to be a Difference Maker!

1
Philippians 4:19

2
Matthew 6:31-33

3
Luke 12:24

4
Psalm 34:10

5
Psalm 145:15-16

FAVOR

"The earth is the LORD's, and everything in it,
the world, and all who live in it;
for He founded it on the seas
and established it on the waters"
(Psalm 24:1-2).
God is the Creator of the heaven and earth. He owns the world and all that is in it. This means that He is
Alive!
Well!
At work within His creation.
He's called the "Invisible God" (1 Timothy 1:17).
The LORD is not sitting idly by watching things unfold in the world.
His grace and favor are extended upon people in the earth.
The Bible says He goes through the earth looking for His children to show His favor to,
"For the eyes of the LORD range throughout the earth to strengthen those whose hearts are fully committed to him..."
(2 Chronicles 16:9, NIV).

Have you ever heard a sermon that was speaking directly to your circumstance?
Have you ever had a person speak a kind word or show you a favor you didn't earn?
Have you experienced a miracle when you didn't know how it was going to work out?
Have you ever received a blessing that you did not ask for?

These are examples of God's favor.
God's favor opens doors you can't open for yourself.
God's favor is Him showing up in a tangible way, expressing His love for you and for the earth.
When you woke up this morning did you see the sun rise?
When you walked outside did you feel the cool wind on your skin?
Did you feel the warmth of the sun?
Did you cuddle your beloved pet?
Did you kiss the one you love?
All of this is an extension of God's favor.
It's the essence of His love that allows us to experience His favor.
These expressions of love reflect the beauty of the LORD.

Seek God's favor daily by seeking His face.
To seek His face means to seek to know who He is.
When you know Him, you'll smile a lot and live in divine blessings. You will never fail!

"May the favor of the LORD our God rest on us;
establish the work of our hands for us—
yes, establish the work of our hands"
(Psalm 90:17).

DEAR

ELIJAH

Write a one-page letter to Elijah sharing how his life inspires you. Share what you've learned from his example and how he's encouraged you to be a Difference Maker in your home, school and community.

DIFFERENCE MAKER MINDSET

THINK. BE. CONNECT. DO.

A DIFFERENCE MAKER IS...

A boy and man who eagerly works with his hands (using his passions, energy, talents and gifts) to serve his community, shining the light of Christ into the world.

A Difference Maker Mindset is a boy and man who is connected to God and knows His will. He looks for opportunities then actively uses his passions, energy, talents and gifts to honor God and love and serve others.

DM
DIFFERENCE MAKER

Think like Christ.

Be like Christ.

Connect with Believers.

Do God's work in the Earth.

Difference Makers are the Body of Christ

"Now you are the body of Christ and each one of you is a part of it"
(1 Corinthians 12:27, NIV).

To be a Difference Maker you have to think like one. When you think like one you become it. You become a Difference Maker before you do anything. What you think in your heart is who you are. When you believe in your heart that God has called you to impact your community for good, then you can do what Difference Makers do.

Think like a
Difference Maker.

Believe you are a
Difference Maker.

Do what Difference
Makers do.

Life of a Difference Maker:
Regular Prayer and Fasting.
Regular Prayer.
Reading and Knowing God's Word.
Faith in Action.
Community Service.
Regular Fellowship with Believers.
Living Righteously by Imitating the Image of Christ.
Experiencing Joy, Peace, Hope and Love.

You are not alone in this faith journey. There are many other Difference Makers called "believers" in your local Church community and all around the world. Your Church community is also called the "body of Christ." The Bible tells us its important to spend time with others who believe in Jesus. You can receive encouragement, support, friendship, love and growth in your faith. Believers and fellow Difference Makers can serve with you to accomplish God's will.

Check out the next page, "Difference Makers are God's Chosen People" to learn the next steps to living the lifestyle of a believer.

DIFFERENCE MAKERS ARE GOD'S CHOSEN PEOPLE

Difference Makers are God's Chosen People, a Holy Nation.
Difference Makers are and do the following based on 1 Peter 2:1-25
(Read and study the additional scriptures added):

- Get rid of these sins: deceit (fraud, cheating), malice (meanness, cruelty), hypocrisy (falseness, acting differently with different people at different places and times), envy (jealousy, grudge) and slander (talking bad about others).

- Like a newborn baby crave spiritual milk, which is the word of God, the Bible so you can grow up in salvation. Salvation is being saved by God through Jesus Christ from sin, death and eternal separation from God.

- You are being built into spiritual houses to be a royal priesthood. A spiritual house is a symbol for believers who are the temple of the Holy Spirit (1 Corinthian 6:19). The Church makes up the LORD's temple. Each believer is a living stone of the building with Christ as the cornerstone (the centerpiece the Church is built upon).

- A royal priesthood Is God's chosen people, a holy nation and God's special possession. You are chosen to declare the praises of Him who called you out of darkness into His wonderful light.

- You offer spiritual sacrifices acceptable to God through Jesus Christ, "Spiritual sacrifices include the believer's prayers, praises, will, bodies, time, and talents. Such sacrifices are made acceptable to God only through Jesus Christ, the great High Priest" (Got Questions Ministries, 2022, para. 3).

- Hold Jesus as the cornerstone who is precious, always making Him the center of your work and worship.

- Trust in the LORD and you will never be put to shame.

- Receive mercy.

DIFFERENCE MAKERS ARE GOD'S CHOSEN PEOPLE CONT.

- You abstain from sinful desires that wage war against your soul (1 Peter 2:11).
- Live a good life among unbelievers so they may see your good deeds and glorify God.
- Submit to human authority for the LORD's sake which includes emperors and governors, honoring the emperor.
- Doing good silences the ignorant talk of foolish people.
- Live as free people but don't use your freedom as a cover-up for evil.
- Live as God's slaves which means "servants", "doing His good, perfect and pleasing will" (Romans 12:2, NIV).
- Show respect to everyone.
- Love the family of believers.
- Fear (respect) God.
- Suffer for doing good because Christ suffered for you.
- Do not retaliate, threaten or insult back.
- Die to sin and live righteously because by His wounds you are healed.
- The LORD Jesus is the Shepherd and Overseer of your soul, therefore go to Him for all spiritual guidance and life direction (Psalm 23).

A Difference Maker serves their community and models a godly lifestyle as written in 1 Peter 2: 1-25.

ARMOR OF GOD

Serving God requires putting on the full armor of God.
Read Ephesians 6:10-20.
Each piece of armor is listed below. Write the action Paul instructs you to take with each piece of the armor.

- [ ] The Belt of Truth- Stand firm with the belt of truth buckled around my waist.
- [ ] The Breastplate of Righteousness
- [ ] The Shield of Faith
- [ ] The Sword of the Spirit
- [ ] The Helmet of Salvation
- [ ] Fitted with the Gospel of Peace
- [ ] Pray in the Spirit on all occasions.
- [ ] Be alert to not fall into the devils wicked schemes.
- [ ] Always pray for the LORD's people, fellow Difference Makers.

YOU ARE GIFTED!

God has gifted you with many gifts and talents to fulfill His will in the earth.
Your gifts and talents are an indication of your purpose.
We volunteer and work in jobs or careers based on our interests, hobbies, passions, gifts and talents. If you need help completing this worksheet do a web search for free personality tests, spiritual gift assessments and inventories. For boys, search for these specifically for kids.
This is the time to do self-exploration! Take your time to complete this worksheet, there's no rush.

Natural Gifts-inherent (built-in) talents you have at birth.

Spiritual Gifts-supernatural abilities given by the Holy Spirit to benefit the Church and further God's kingdom. Go back to page 71 discussion question #2 where you listed spiritual gifts. Use spiritual gift inventories online to help you answer this question. There are free ones available.

Talents-skills developed through practice.

Interests-activities and topics that excite; you want to know more about them.
Hobbies-activities and topics you do in your leisure time for your pleasure.
Passions-intensely desiring to do something

FAITH IN ACTION: COMMUNITY SERVICE

Now you've identified your gifts, talents, interests, hobbies, and passions its time to serve your community. Research five areas of need in your community and the organizations offering opportunities for you to use your gifts, talents or work within your hobbies, interests and passions.
For example: feeding the poor, serving the elderly, volunteering in children's ministry at your local Church, mentoring boys and teens, picking up trash, cutting hair, teaching a skill to others, farming, yard work, singing, acting, technology, science, volunteering in places of government or social work.

Example
1 -Area of need
Children's Ministry

2- Who's in need?
Children of my Church

3-Organization Name
My Local Church

4-How can I help?
Volunteer 1-2 times a month in the newborn class.

1 - Area of Need

2-Who's in need?

3-Organization Name

4-How can I help?

1 - Area of Need

2-Who's in need?

3-Organization Name

4-How can I help?

1 - Area of Need

2-Who's in need?

3-Organization Name

4-How can I help?

1 - Area of Need

2-Who's in need?

3-Organization Name

4-How can I help?

1 - Area of Need

2-Who's in need?

3-Organization Name

4-How can I help?

MY DIFFERENCE MAKER CHECKLIST

Now that you've identified where you can use your gifts and talents its time to put your faith into action. This checklist has standard things you can do to get started serving your community. There is a second sheet on the next page for you to make your own checklist. Next, is the planning stage. You've been supplied with a weekly, one month, three month and six month planner to help you continue to map out the steps to putting your faith into action. Use these planners however you want to organize your thoughts, time and energy. Let's get to work Difference Maker!

- [ ] Contact the organization.
- [ ] Complete applications or forms, if necessary.
- [ ] Schedule a day to meet with staff or volunteers.
- [ ] Plan how long your commitment will be.
- [ ] Schedule the day of service.
- [ ] Serve.
- [ ]
- [ ]
- [ ]

MY DIFFERENCE MAKER CHECKLIST

Now that you've identified where you can use your gifts and talents its time to put your faith into action. This checklist is for you to log your steps of getting started volunteering with the ministry or community organization of your choice. Let's get to work Difference Maker!

- [ ]
- [ ]
- [ ]
- [ ]
- [ ]
- [ ]
- [ ]
- [ ]

WEEKLY PLANNER

Monday

Tuesday

Wednesday

Thursday

Friday

Saturday

Sunday

ONE MONTH PLANNER

WEEK ONE

WEEK TWO

WEEK THREE

WEEK FOUR

WEEK FIVE

NOTES

THREE MONTH PLANNER

MONTH ONE **MONTH TWO** **MONTH THREE**

NOTES

____
____
____
____
____
____
____
____

NOTES

____
____
____
____
____
____
____
____

SIX MONTH PLANNER

MONTH ONE

MONTH TWO

MONTH THREE

MONTH FOUR

MONTH FIVE

MONTH SIX

PLANNING PAGE

Extra page for planning and keeping notes.

ITS TIME TO WRITE YOUR OWN IRONCLAD LETTER!

Now that you have the Difference Maker Mindset its time to complete your own letter on the next page.

Maybe this is the first time or a review but it's time to celebrate yourself!

This letter hopefully gives insight into the following:

Who you are.

What makes you unique.

What your strong traits are.

What your gifts, talents, interests, hobbies and passions are.

Take what you already know about yourself and the inspiration from the other ironclad men to create your own letter.

Enjoy!

LETTER ELEVEN

Write your name here.

Instructions: On this page complete the Building Character section first then the top section of this page. Look back at other letters as a guide.

WRITE YOUR NAME ABOVE

SERVED THE COMMUNITY AS:

Write a short statement or two to three words describing how you currently serve your community or what you want to do in the future to serve your community.

Strong Traits:

Write three of your strongest traits and qualities that make you unique.

__________________ **name meaning:**

Write your name and research it's meaning.

Lesson/My life in one day:

What lesson can people learn from looking at your life? If you need to develop this answer over time, do so. There's no rush.

If you had one day to do an act of kindness what you would do?

Write one trait in each box. Write the definition.

Building Character: Being more like Jesus

This is your opportunity to study the life of Jesus. His ministry is recorded in the New Testament books of Matthew, Mark, Luke and John. Choose one of these books to study then answer the questions as a guide to prepare you to write a letter of inspiration to yourself. Here are some suggestions for Jesus' stories you could use in this section for inspiration: Matthew 14:13-21, Matthew 19:13-14, Luke 13:11-13, John 5:1-18.

Name of person(s) (if he/she doesn't have a name write what the Bible calls him/her) Jesus impacted, loved and served:

Bible chapter and verses of the story:

List three traits that make you unique. These can be traits you already see within yourself or traits you see in Jesus that you want to imitate. At the top of this page write your traits in the "strong traits" section.

How did Jesus serve the community? Write your answer on the Notes page. For Ironclad boys ages 11-13 see page 112.
These questions are guiding questions to help you answer, "How did Jesus serve the community?" They all do not have to be answered. If you can't find the answer, consider doing this with a partner. To answer these questions read the Bible story of your choice about Jesus' ministry from either Matthew, Mark, Luke and John. You may use additional studies such as commentaries to understand the culture and time, but you don't have to.
What did Jesus do or how did He serve the community?
How did Jesus reveal who God was to people? Was there a lesson He was teaching?
Did Jesus perform a miracle? Does the Bible reveal why Jesus blessed that person?
How does Jesus respond in a challenging situation?
How did Jesus represent God in a challenging situation?
How can you imitate Christ in your actions?
How did Jesus lead people to faith in Himself?
The answer to all these questions may not appear in the story but you're encouraged to use your critical thinking skills. These are just a guide to helping you look into the Bible story and answer the question "How did Jesus serve the community?"

AN IRONCLAD MAN IS...

Write a summary on how your traits are displayed when you're living your life or serving your community and glorifying God. You can also write how you'd want to display your traits in the future.

Write your three strong traits above.

List each trait. Research and write at least one scripture that reflects each trait.

READ EACH VERSE. **WRITE THE SCRIPTURES IN THE BLANK SPACE.**

Trait One:

Trait Two:

Trait Three:

Note section for additional scriptures or what you've learned while studying.

NOTES

- How did Jesus serve His community in the Bible story you chose? What good thing did Jesus do in the Bible story? How was God pleased with Jesus? How did Jesus use love to serve other people? Write your answers on your notes page.

NOTES

I SERVE/I WILL SERVE MY COMMUNITY...

Write up to a one-page compilation of everything you've learned about yourself and how you plan to use what you've learn to serve your community. If what you have to say is more than one-page, page 112 has been provided.
Review the Difference Maker Mindset section, noting your gifts, talents, interests, hobbies and passions.
Review the "A Ironclad Man Is...", noting your traits.
Review your "How did Jesus serve the community?" notes to complete this page.
Focus on how you can serve within the next 30 days. There is no right or wrong way to complete this section.
This is for you to encourage yourself.

I SERVE/I WILL SERVE MY COMMUNITY...

Write your name is the space above. Write a one-page letter encouraging yourself. Write how your life inspires others or how it will in the future. Write what you've learned about yourself. Write how you are already a Difference Maker in your home, school and community or how you see yourself becoming one.

DEAR

OPTIONAL: Share this letter with another boy, young man/man so he can write an encouraging letter to you. Then find a fellow Ironclad Man and write a letter in his workbook. Letter writer: You don't have to know someone personally to write a blessing to them. You can write a general letter to him blessing him to be and do well as he lives in Christ. If you do know this person write how he's inspirational or will inspire others in the future.

DEAR IRONCLAD MAN,

YOU ARE A DIFFERENCE MAKER. GO INTO THE WORLD AND SHINE FOR CHRIST!

I hope this study led you to learning yourself and your capabilities but most importantly learning more about God and His capabilities when you surrender to Him. I hope this study enriched, empowered, humbled, lifted you up and set you on fire for your future; for what the LORD will do through you.

I pray this study sparked within you a lifetime celebration of yourself and the uniqueness that you bring so you serve your home, school and community in volunteer work, in the workplace and in business with greatness!
Let the things you've learned about God extend to how you see yourself, creating a partnership between you and God to impact your community for the glory of His name now and in the future.

Keep thinking, connecting, being and doing!

Blessings,

Crystal

References

Got Questions Ministries. (2022, January 4). What are spiritual sacrifices. Got Questions. https://www.gotquestions.org/spiritual-sacrifices.html.

Merriam-Webster. (n.d.). Ironclad. In Merriam-Webster.com dictionary. Retrieved April 15, 2026, from https://www.merriam-webster.com/dictionary/ironclad.

New International Version. (2011). Bible Gateway. https://www.biblegateway.com/versions/New-International-Version-NIV-Bible/.

www.ingramcontent.com/pod-product-compliance
Lightning Source LLC
LaVergne TN
LVHW061204120826
845149LV00011B/1900

* 9 7 9 8 9 9 4 7 9 8 6 2 1 *